OPERA ET CETERA

CIARAN CARSON

Opera Et Cetera

BLOODAXE BOOKS

ISBN: 1 85224 396 1

First published 1996 by
Bloodaxe Books Ltd,
P.O. Box 1SN,
Newcastle upon Tyne NE99 1SN.

Published simultaneously in Ireland
by The Gallery Press.

Bloodaxe Books Ltd acknowledges
the financial assistance of Northern Arts.

Cover printing by J. Thomson Colour Printers Ltd, Glasgow.

Printed in Great Britain by
Cromwell Press Ltd, Broughton Gifford, Melksham, Wiltshire.

Contents

for Manus, Gerard and Mary

Eesti

I wandered homesick-lonely through that Saturday of
    silent Tallinn
When a carillon impinged a thousand raining quavers
    on my ear, tumbling

Dimly from immeasurable heights into imaginary brazen
    gong-space, trembling
Dimpled in their puddled, rain-drop halo-pools,
    concentrically assembling.

I glimpsed the far-off, weeping onion-domes. I was
    inveigled towards the church
Through an aural labyrinth of streets until I sheltered
    in its porch.

I thumbed the warm brass worn thumb-scoop of the latch.
    Tock. I entered into bronze-
Dark, shrines and niches lit by beeswax tapers and
    the sheen of ikons.

Their eyes and the holes in their hands were nailed into
    my gaze, quod erat demonstrandum:
Digits poised and pointed towards their hearts. They
    are beautiful Panjandrums

Invoked by murmuring and incense, hymns that father
    passes on to father,
The patina of faces under painted faces. They evoke
    another

Time, where I am going with you, father, to first Mass.
    We walked
The starry frozen pavement, holding hands to stop
    ourselves from falling. There was no talk,

Nor need for it. Our incense-breath was words enough
  as we approached the Gothic,
Shivering in top-coats, on the verge of sliding off
  the metronomic

Azure-gradual dawn, as nave and transept summoned us
  with beaded, thumbed
And fingered whispering. Silk-tasselled missals.
  Rosaries. Statues stricken dumb

Beneath their rustling purple shrouds, as candles
  wavered in the holy smoke.
The mosaic chapel echoed with a clinking, chinking
  censer-music.

This red-letter day would not be written, had I not
  wandered through the land of Eesti.
I asked my father how he thought it went. He said to
  me in Irish, Listen: Éist.

LETTERS
FROM THE
ALPHABET

for Leon McAuley

A

Invisible to radar, *Stealth* glided through their retina
     of sweep and dot.
No bleep appeared to register its Alpha wing. The watchers
     were asleep, or not.

An Ampoule-bomb lay Ampère-wired-up in it, waiting for
     its primal sec-
Ond, like its embryonic *A* becoming *Be*. It wanted flash
     and Instamatic.

Its crew is snorkelled into oxygen, and getting high as
     kites. Its eagle eye
Zooms in and out across the infra-red. Its map is
     virtual reality:

O porcelain metropolis, inlaid with palaces of majuscule
     Baroque
And Trojan *equus* statues; fountains, spices, frozen music,
     gardens, oranges from Maroc!

I put my feet into the crew's shoes, my hands into
     their gloves, and felt the chill
Of borrowed armour. My *a priori* gauntlet twitched and
     hit the button: *Kill.*

B

I buzzed on to the screen invisibly, like *the second
    hypothetical
Person or example*, like I was a tab of mescaline, heretical.

Like an aspirin dot, I flitted through the frames of
    twenty-four-a-second *noir*;
Through amber fog and urban streets I drove a minuscule
    of scarab-armoured car.

I crawled, blue-bottle-green, across the drive-in
    window-pane. I dithered on
Its glass. I was a sound like 78s or engines revving off,
    diminuendo on.

Then His Master flipped the Twenties record over on
    its second shellac back
And listened to the hiss of bumbled opera, revolving from
    the archaic black.

Fluffy was the needle-dust. He scraped it with the
    callus of his thumb.
He grooved it in again. The clockwork clucked and tutted.
    The orchestra went dumb.

C

We have this plan, because if all else fails, we will
    rehearse its contemplated moves
Again, as argent beings of the horse-men are contingent
    on their hooves

Plunged into a fully-moonlit destination. It's the
    crescent
Elvis paring of the King's big toe-nail, like a snipped-
    off tense of present.

It's the belle who found it, hoovering on hands and
    knees behind the Cadillac-
Sized king bed-head. It's the overpowering smell of
    diapers and lilac.

So I stuck another candle in the purblind cataract
    of wax;
I pronounced the little *see* in *incense* as I said a
    prayer for *pax*.

I felt like the clunk of the coin as it dropped
    through the slot of the box: dark
Reliquary, from which I glimpsed the moon, the
    fingernail, the scimitar.

D

Whoever takes an arrow to this bow will really feel
    the slippery sap
Of the freshly-peeled sally-rod and the tensile spring
    of the future slap

Of the string, all imaginary targets riddled through
    with past plu-
Perfect hits and misses; the lucky shot of two birds
    skewered in the perfect blue.

All thumbs and fingers tweezerlike, I unbarbed his
    fletcher's herringbone,
Like I unstuck the hoops and loops of the Velcro
    Celtic Twilight Zone.

I unzipped it open, and so witnessed the opposing oars
    of quinquereme
And decked-out trireme, how they rowed majestically
    into Byzantium:

A shower of arrows welcomed them like needles to a
    magnet, like the whole
Assault of future into present, the way that the South
    attracts the North pole.

E

E is the teeth of the bit on the end of the shank
    of a key
Which Carter fits into the keyhole ankh of Tutankhamun's
    reliquary.

It's like he put the *ka* in *karaoke*, or his A-side
    met his Doppel-
Gänger B and shook hands with himself, saying,
    Sorry for your trouble.

The stylus ticked and ticked like it was stuck in one
    groove of eternity. The disc-
Warp wobbled, river-dark and vinyl-shiny. Dust was in
    its Lethe dusk.

The noiseless E-type black Felucca came for him across
    the water.
It was automatic. The back door opened up. The other
    Carter sat beside his mater.

Carter joined Carter. It was a crux of matter. She
    handed him the hip-flask.
He drank. *Where are we going, mater?* She drew her veil.
    She sealed his lips. *Don't ask.*

F

F stands for forceps, or rather a wrench with adjustable
    jaws. I rubbed
The milled-edge Zippo callus on my thumb, and felt
    that everything was dubbed:

The *mise en scène*, the plot, the lines, the jokey
    thumb-and-finger 'money' signs,
The way a lucifer flared up, illuminating dark
    conspirators' designs,

Who are mostly Trojan shadows, adumbrated in the
    lens of infra-red,
Or bugs reverberating with the buzz of what was overheard
    and said.

He switched it off. *This is the spanner in the works?*
    The word? The horse's mouth?
I said it was ineffable. I'd bought the dope from guys
    who knew its worth.

Hector looked into its larynx and agreed the tapes
    had been secreted.
The forceps president resigned. His oratorical
    expletives were deleted.

G

His hand had been clamped in a G-clamp to the Black
    & Decker work-bench.
Claw-head hammers, pincers, lost-head nails: they said
    it was the work of *Untermensch*.

Meanwhile, G-men trawled the underworld with darkened
    retinas and double-
Breasted trench coats. Shook hands at funerals, saying,
    Sorry for your trouble.

Meanwhile, bugs proliferated all across the city:
    gnats, gads, gargle-flies and gall-flies
Spawned from entomology of G; they laid their eggs
    in gigabits in data-banks and files of lies.

Meanwhile, they took in the buzz in the bar through
    the radio-blue-bottle-lens,
As 'Black' told 'Decker' what had really *sotto voce*
    happened. The bits they got made sense:

Meanwhile, his hand has been clamped in the jaws of
    a vice to the work-bench.
X *and* Y *are dissecting the best approach to the work.*
    X *picks up a wrench.*

H

The Powers-that-Be decreed that from the — of ———
    the sausage rolls, for reasons
Of security, would be contracted to a different firm.
    They gave the prisoners no reasons.

The prisoners complained. We cannot reproduce his actual
    words here, since their spokesman is alleged
To be a sub-commander of a movement deemed to be illegal.

An actor spoke for him in almost-perfect lip-synch:
    It's not the quality
We're giving off about. Just that it seems they're
    getting smaller. We're talking quantity.

His 'Belfast' accent wasn't West enough. Is the *H*
    in H-Block *aitch* or *haitch*?
Does it matter? *What we have we hold? Our day will come?*
    Give or take an inch?

Well, give an inch and someone takes an effing mile.
    Everything is in the ways
You say them. Like, the prison that we call Long Kesh
    is to the Powers-that-Be *The Maze.*

I

I is the vertical, the virtual reality. I tell it slant.
I am leaning into you to nudge you. I am Immanuel,
    and you are Kant.

I have been around so long, I have the memory of an
    elephant;
Although I think that I deserve some praise, I hope
    you're not a sycophant.

I am Sherlock Holmes and you are Watson. And if you're
    not, you are my client.
You are cocaine, I am the nose. You walk straight and
    narrow. I am deviant.

I be the bow and you be the fiddle. You will always be
    compliant.
I am the hinge of language, you its door. I think
    you understand my cant.

I am karaoke, you the guy with the mike. I am plain-
    chant, you are descant.
When I think, I think I am. But when I have you, what
    do I want?

J

The calligraphic *1* of 19— is close to it, as I
    transcribed it in the ring-
Bound half-morocco stamp album in my early teens.
    It's not the *Ding*

An sich, for everything is *ad hoc*: what was I doing
    writing this, all those aeons
Ago — *13 Nov. 1941, Centenary of Announcement of*
    Discovery of Quaternions?

Or, *5 Dec. 1949, 100th Anniversary of J. C. Mangan's*
    Death?
I took it out of catalogues, of course, the way that
    Aleph leads to Beth.

Or, two musicians are cutting turf. *A* asks the other, *B*,
    for a reel he half-
Remembers. The other takes his J-spade. In the bank
    of turf he cuts a staff.

Then the notes. O'Keeffe was one of them. I think
    the other was a Murph.
Of course the notes are not the tune. The tune itself
    they called 'The Bank of Turf'.

K

K is the leader of the empty orchestra of karaoke.
K is the conductor on the wrong bus that you took today
    and landed you in yesterday

Where everything was skew. The rainbow colours were
    all out of kilter,
Like oil had leaked out all over the road from a dropped
    and broken philtre.

There, no one wanted to be recognised, and walked
    around in wrap-round
Polaroids. There was Semtex in the Maxwell House,
    and twenty shillings in the pound.

K came into it again, with the sidelong, armed stance
    of a Pharaoh.
He took my kopeck, docked it with two holes, and told
    me it was time to go.

All the motor-cars were black. I got behind the wheel
    of one. It worked O.K.
Welder's sparks zipped from the trolley. The radio
    was playing karaoke.

L

I'm always sitting in the wrong corner of the room
        or in the wrong angle,
So that part of it is hidden from me always. Like
        you are in the ingle-

Nook and I am not, or you are upstairs ironing. I
        can nearly hear the hiss
As the *Sunbeam* hits the aromatic damp of cloth. It's like
        a breathy kiss,

The warm snog of a freshly-pressed cotton shirt I
        put on for the interview.
Like, I don't know who's upright, who is horizontal.
        But the *L* is me and you.

As the ironing board remembers it, it bears a burnt
        Sienna scorch
Of memory. For all its *this* and *that* and *is* and *was*
        it carries a torch.

I felt like the girl in a hairdresser's, flicking backwards
        through an issue of *Elle*,
As it gets dark outside. A momentary train passed by
        with lighted windows on the El.

M

When *M* is amplified among the gongs and incense, it
   becomes an *om*
Resounding in the saffron gloom. Smoke rises up as if
   from meerschaum.

It's a sort of unusual Vermeer, with pewter mugs and
   dogs drunk under
The table. Hanging from the ceiling is a caged *macaco*
   monkey, ponder-

Ing the digits of her basic American Sign Language
   for *nuts*. They bring
Her beer instead. Outside, on the icy mere, the
   families are skating.

It is beautiful to breathe the civic, clean, cold-
   stone-sober air after all that smoke,
To see the skated babies slithering around in Babygros
   under older folk,

While in the artist's back yard, drawers and bras
   and shirts and pinafores are fro-
Zen on a line; stiffened overnight, they're creaking
   to and fro.

N

I am a dash or a void. It's up to you to make me up.
    Wake up,
You, the reader! I have some tales to tell you, and
    the night is but a pup.

I was Nemo once, a kind of Prospero. When I imbibed
    a bit of Bob,
My Nameless One became His Nibs, an eponymous
    proper Nabob.

Of course, my nadirs have been various: *Electric Ray
    the Numbfish*,
For example. He was really nesh. Those jokes about
    the actress and the Bish?

Still, I am a nebula: my lives illuminate their
    dazzling firmament;
Innumerable stars gaze down at you, as if they really
    meant.

You mean you smoked a bit of dope? The names of
    things have gone all AWOL?
Listen to me. Nemo is not a nobody. And *Nautilus*
    is not a narwhal.

O

The tea-cup stain on the white damask table-cloth was
    not quite perfect. Never-
Theless, I'd set my cup exactly on it, like it was a stain-
    remover.

I sipped the rim with palatable lip. I drank the steaming
    liquor up.
My granny then would read my future from the tea-leaves'
    leavings in the cup.

I stared into enormous china O and saw its every
    centrifugal flaw,
The tiny bobbles glazed in its interior of Delphic
    oracle. I yawned

Into its incandescent blaze of vowel like the cool of
    dudes in black fedoras
At high noon; trigger-fingered, shadowless, they walked
    beneath sombreros.

They stopped me inadvertently and asked for my identity.
    I did not know
Until the mouth of a gun was pressed against my forehead,
    and I felt its O.

P

Let *p* be a logical palabra, opposing itself to *q*,
Thus: a Pyrex bowl is not the Christmas pudding steaming in it;
   pea is not a *cue*.

You can imagine the scene: Holmes and Watson, Pee and
    Queue, have disembarked
From the dog-cart. They have gone into the gloomy Hall.
   Inside is a time-warp.

The statues were all wrapped and swaddled. A log fire
    bubbles, spits and cracks;
The rattled Pyrex is an intermittent dither in the
    background. It's the crux

Of why Lord —— was beaten to death in the billiard
    room with a snooker cue,
Of how he lay petrified, undiscovered until Boxing Day,
    of why the statue

Of himself had been removed. Holmes sucked his meerschaum.
    Puffs of shaggy smoke
Were intermittent as he said, *The proof is in the pudding.*
    Then Watson spoke:

Q

Q is useless without its *u* except in narcotic cases
    like qat.
You stick a bunch of leaves in your cheek and chew:
    it's an elaborate

Social ritual too. The French gunrunner Arthur Rimbaud
    is said to have par-
Taken of it, especially when he felt a little bit under
    par:

I am an ephemeral and not at all too-discontented
    citizen
Of a metropolis where hashish has pacified the wild
    assassin . . .

The dope, the grass, the speed, the smack, the junk,
    the weed, the blow, the crack
Illuminated him. His *O* was blue, his *I* was red, his
    A was black:

Then a little daughter put a squiggly *o* on top of
    Q to make a cat;
She looked at it, then put a pair of wings on it, and
    said, *That's bat.*

R

I love the shape of an *R*: its curve, its upright and
    its flying buttress.
When it is amplified, it is the warble-thunder of a
    Flying Fortress.

I saw it crissed and crossed by ack-ack battery torches
    in the war theatre.
I'd assembled it from *Airfix*. High on glue, I was
    its aviator

Or the tiny gunner in the Perspex bubble swivel turret,
    trigger-
Fingered. Below us lay the woven Persian contoured
    abstract Paisley figures.

The sky was an unreachable ceiling, where Spitfire-flies
    buzzed lazily
Around the sun. The ocean was brown lino, imagined into
    lapis lazuli.

Sometimes I'd curl into an armchair continent and gaze
    at my creations:
Heinkel, Stuka, Messerschmitt, like words an orator
    resounds in empty amphitheatres.

S

The train slowed to a halt with a sigh like *Schweppes*.
    I see you now, Miranda,
Through the glassed-in cloudy steam of yesteryear. Do
    you remember, Miranda,

The archaic of when I met you first, that time when all
    the motor-cars were black?
My heartache? I did not stand out from the crowd, I was
    a stand-in in a claque.

And you were Carmen, Miranda, you were Madama Butterfly.
    You were prox-
Opera, the roles that you insinuated into. And you knew
    you were it. Those parox-

Ysms of grief! Those swooning cadences! Those rolling
    eyes and *R*s! The spotlight
Kissed you as the claque went crazy, hurling flowers and
    lire at you. It was out of sight.

And I was there, Miranda, in the empty theatre, picking
    up your petals. I walked on plush.
I felt I was the silent *s* in *aisle*. And where were you,
    Miranda? *Hush*.

T

T is *tea*, which is what they used to call grass or dope
    or smoke or blow.
It's the junction of minor and major roads. Its amber's
    neither stop nor go.

It's the bitten amber mouthpiece of the unsmoked
    meerschaum in the pipe-rack.
It's the tin of *Mick McQuaid* tobacco, the *psst* as
    you prise its blue lid and the vac-

Uum escapes; it's the pungent, urgent, aromatic whiff
    of nicotine.
I unblossomed it and rubbed it. I tamped it down into
    the bowl. I lit it with a *Mezzanine* —

You remember those old-fashioned lucifers that came
    in a yellow matchwood box?
The sulphur, bulbous, rose-bud red of their tips?
    You know, the equinox

Of when we talked, and you were smoking Passing Clouds?
    That *dim sum* place, whatever
It was called? The silly names we gave each other?
    No? 'The Twelfth of Never'?

U

The urchin is a hedgehog, hence its corallaceous spines.
    It's made its *U*
Into a balled-up Erinacean *O* of Rimbaud green or blue,
    depending how you

See it. It is a self-protective device, like the
    independent eye
Of the chameleon, or the stripes on a zebra crossing.
    It's the amber eye

Of the traffic lights. It's a corona — not Havana, but
    the sound-horn
Of a daffodil, emitting blue stars from its halo crown
    of thorns.

If you drive over one, it gets squashed, so you often
    come across
Them flattened, parchment-like on rural roads, especially
    in poems like this.

Their *Zeitgeist* is reverse, if *verse* means *the turn at*
    the end of a furrow.
They propagate themselves by not eating their own
    farrow.

V

To gouge out, as the eye with the thumb. To signal
　　Victory, or *Up yours.*
To take a detour to the Vee-Dub rally, where Beetles
　　droned around for hours.

To puff through the valley. To listen to the murmuring
　　inversion of its stream
In mill-wheels. To appreciate its Alpine air and rack-
　　and-pinion antiquated steam

Train. To feel the locomotive cinder in your eye, to
　　smell the coal-smoke.
To be soaring on the cranky ski-lift. To see the snow
　　as white as coke.

Like an avalanche, infinitive comes into it and buries
　　me
Diurnally beneath itself in wave of verb and rock and
　　stone and tree.

I ended up embodied in the glacier: my frozen
　　outstretched *I*
Stared out at me, like the *v* in *Balaklava*, all wool
　　and mouth and eyes.

W

I call you Double You. You, you wouldn't know your
    yin from *yang*, nor one side
Of a Doppelgänger baseball from the other. You think
    your curve's a slide.

Well, I'm willing to believe you, for I think I know
    ambivalence, the double
Vale of Tears where cataracts plunge into pools of
    logo-bubble.

The iridescent globe is frail: you blow it, then I
    touch it and it van-
Ishes, all its wobbly gliding gone, an instant after
    it began.

Or I see you in some gondola, slowly soaring, slung
    beneath your air balloon,
Your buoyant gas that takes my vision to the stratosphere,
    the hunter's moon

Which you're a drifting speck against, like something
    in my eye. I rubbed it
And I saw the constellation *W*; or Cassiopeia, as some
    astronomer has dubbed it.

X

I dipped my fingertips into the font of stone-cold,
    heavy water
And felt a volt of tingle up my spine. She asked
    what was the Ampère matter.

It froze me to the bone, her lapidary, *volte-face*-like
    Marian blue
Becoming flesh. She unstoned her mummy lips and spoke
    unlike a statue.

Of Nobel and of Molotov she drawled, of atom bombs
    and Coulomb
Interactions. She broached the suture of the future
    with aplomb.

She ripped the bandage off my eyes. Elastoplast, it
    made a Velcro
Kind of zip. What before was monochrome and mezzotint
    was Day-Glo.

She thrust my fontanelle into the font of stone-cold-
    sober imprimatur.
Stet. She crossed me out. She left me with the empty
    ampoule of Lourdes water.

Y

It's only now that I recall the catapult I cut from
    the ash tree,
How I bound with wire to the tangs of its fork an
    elastic strip snipped out free-

Hand from a long-deflated inner tube. Not to forget
    the leather thing-
Amajig for holding the stone or whatever. I guess you
    call it the sling.

But the sling is, I think, the elastic too. There
    must be a language of slang,
Some children's twang where words hit home, dit-dah,
    to the Auld Lang

Syne of what they were, and why. As if the marble shot
    had boomeranged
And got you right between the teeth, just to remind
    you it was no meringue.

Still, I try to bite into it. Then I did. Nothing
    happened. I thought on,
A thong of stretched elastic swish. Then I hit the
    recall button.

Z

The ultimate buzz is the sound of sleep or of bees,
    or the slalom I'll
Make through the dark pines of a little-known Alp
    on my snowmobile.

You will hear me fading and droning towards you from
    the valley next
To one, for I have miles to go: when I deliver all the
    letters, that's the text.

The canvas sack on my back reminds me I am in the
    archaic footprints
Of my postman father. I criss and cross the zig-zag
    precedents.

Snow is falling fast, my parallels already blurring
    on the mountainside,
But I am flying towards you through the stars on
    skis of Astroglide.

In the morning you will open up the envelope. You
    will get whatever
Message is inside. It is for all time. Its postmark
    is 'The Twelfth of Never'.

ET CETERA

Auditque Vocatus Apollo

We were climbing Parnassus. My guide kept asking
    me 'how a man can
Penetrate through the lyre's strings'. I tried to think
    of a silly answer, and a can-

Can dancer's disembodied legs sprang to mind, or the
    patent ostrich-egg-
Slicer of a harp. *Our mind*, he said, *is split*. Too
    true. Like he was Quee and I was Queg —

One of those guys. Orpheus. Apollo. Rilke. Ahab. Dick.
    And climbing Mount
Olympia is like that: enquiring for the whale that
    disappears beneath its fount-

Ain spray. You think you've reached the summit when
    another distant crest
Appears to challenge you. *Quo vadis?* Something like that.
    I asked if we could rest.

I don't know why I started this. One summer doesn't
    make a swallow.
Suddenly, the jangling of a lyre. I cried, *Who's there?*
    He says, *It's me. Apollo.*

Solvitur Ambulando

The verse he spoke was like the way he was: those
    bruised blue eyes, the gringo moustache
Flecked with grey, the flat-topped hat, the black
    cheroot with its eternal inch of ash.

The haiku scar in his knee only partly accounted for
    his bow-legged walk;
The rest was many horses, and the monosyllables in which
    he talked

Of nothing much. No one knew his age, nor dared
    to guess his provenance.
He waltzed in black alpaca jacket through the swing
    doors of The Last Chance;

He unbuttoned it and hitched it, showing his two
    hands full of Colts,
Then holstered them again, all this in the noon-struck
    space of two greased lightning bolts.

I was the barkeep under the counter, so I can tell
    you that the story of the song
Is true: *The inch of ash was first to go. The bar was
seventeen steps long.*

Vox et Praeterea Nihil

It sounded right and wet outside, if you believed
    the off-beat window-wiper
Swish-swash variously beyond the drawn blinds, the
    melancholic dim Scotch piper

Tuning-up noise of the far-off traffic jam. I was
    trying to decode
Whatever they'd rehearsed from arbitrary parps
    in Morris Minor mode.

Like the wedding-carillon of limousine and honking
    entourage, the notes
Are always different, though the tune remains the same;
    the 'quotes' are really 'unquotes',

As the campanologists — invariably — are out of synch
    on dangling long
Elastic ropes, though all are trying hard to tell
    their *Ding an sich* from *dong*.

It's not so much the pull, I'm told, but letting go
    that matters, like Sagittarius
With eyes closed, aiming for the bull. That's why
    the same refrain is always various.

Graecum Est: Non Legitur

The fly made an audible syzygy as it dive-bombed
    through the dormer
And made a rendezvous with this, the page I'm writing
    on. It was its karma.

This tsetse was a Greek to me, making wishy-washy
    gestures with its hands
And feet. I made to brush it off, before it vaulted
    off into a handstand

Ceiling-corner of the room. It dithered over to the
    chandelier-flex
And buzzed around it upside down in a stunt-plane
    Camel helix.

The landing-page approached my craft as I began to
    think again. The candle guttered.
My enormous hand was writing on the wall. The words
    began to stutter

As the quill ran out. *Syzygy:* His dizzy Nibs was
    back. I took on board more ink.
He staggered horse-like towards the blue blot I'd
    just dropped. Then he began to drink.

Par Nobile Fratrum

I found George hiding in an angle of his language,
    studying the badge agenda.
'You have to see it through Estonian, with its eighteen
    cases and no gender.'

He had on a gold ring stickpin signifying Irish, plus
    the Esperanto green star.
He had had the Thoughts of Chairman Mao given to him
    by some Jolly Roving Tar

Who'd learned the lingo in Beijing when it was called
    Peking. For years they
Corresponded. George sent him missionary tracts and
    all the Good News hearsay.

Then the other died. I think his name was Chi or Chang.
    At any rate, the widow
Sent George Chang's green star. Or was it Eng? George
    stared out the window:

'If one parent is bilingual, it is absolutely crucial
    not to break
The language bond. I did once, and found it was extremely
    fragile. I have learned by my mistake.'

Jacta Est Alea

It was one of those puzzling necks of the wood where
    the South was in the North, the way
The double cross in a jigsaw loops into its matrix,
    like the border was a *clef*

With arbitrary teeth indented in it. Here, it cut clean
    across the plastic
Lounge of The Half-Way House; my heart lay in
    the Republic

While my head was in the Six, or so I was inclined.
    You know that drinker's
Angle, elbow-propped, knuckles to his brow like one
    of the Great Thinkers?

He's staring at my throat in the Power's mirror,
    debating whether
He should open up a lexicon with me: the price of
    beer or steers, the weather.

We end up talking about talk. We stagger on the frontier.
    He is pro. I am con.
Siamese-like, drunken, inextricable, we wade
    into the Rubicon.

Aquila Non Capit Muscas

Nor does the angel condescend to share our cheese and
    wine, but trapezes
In a daddy-long-legs ceiling-angle: not aloof, not
    partizan,

But mindful of the sacrosanct occasion, *rouge* glugged
    from the neck into our
Necks. The holey Emmental. The drooling Brie. The
    varicose in Roquefort.

It's that picnic weather where we'd wandered from
    the cool of the cathedral
As the Angelus grew dim behind us. We found this spot
    without the city wall

And we were prostrate in a galaxy of buttercups. Principalities
    and Powers
Of flies buzzed round us as we opened up the basket. We
    ate. We dozed for hours.

I dreamt I stalked on yonder far-off blue plateau
    with bullets, gun and beagle,
Abroad for days, enquiring for the Lesser-Spotted
    Fly-catching Eagle.

Cave Quid Dicis, Quando, et Cui

You will recognise them by their Polaroids that make
    the span between their eyes
Immeasurable. Beware their digital watches; they are
    bugged with microscopic batteries.

Make sure you know your left from right and which side
    of the road you walk on.
If one stops beside you and invites you in, do not enter
    the pantechnicon.

You'd be participating in another's house removal.
    You could become
A part of the furniture, slumped in some old armchair.
    That would be unwelcome.

Welcome is the mat that does not spell itself. Words
    don't speak as loud as deeds,
Especially when the safety is off. Watch it if they
    write in screeds,

For everything you say is never lost, but hangs on in
    the starry void
In ghosted thumb-whorl spiral galaxies. Your fingerprints
    are everywhere. *Be paranoid.*

Labuntur et Imputantur

It was overcast. No hour at all was indicated by the
    gnomon.
With difficulty I made out the slogan, *Time and tide*
    wait for no man.

I had been waiting for you, Daphne, underneath the
    dripping laurels, near
The sundial glade where first we met. I felt like Hamlet
    on the parapets of Elsinore,

Alerted to the ectoplasmic moment, when Luna rends
    her shroud of cloud
And sails into a starry archipelago. Then your revenant
    appeared and spake aloud:

I am not who you think I am. For what we used to be
    is gone. The moment's over,
Whatever years you thought we spent together. You don't
    know the story. And moreover,

You mistook the drinking-fountain for a sundial. I put
    my lips to its whatever,
And with difficulty I made out the slogan, *Drink from*
    me and you shall live forever.

Quod Erat Demonstrandum

She was putting together her Cinderella outfit in the
    usual sequin
Sequence she'd bought as pocket galaxies. The headless
    armless mannequin

Was on her mind from yesterday's shop window, as she
    approached her
Doppelgänger in the glass. Suddenly no sisters, as
    the pumpkin coached her

To the ball, drawn by the equine mice. The palace floor
    was disco-glitter stars
She polished, gliding in her fur-soled slippers. The
    Prince, just back from the wars —

Whatever wars they were — escorted her, unscarred by
    his experience.
'He'll make an extremely good king, whatever "being
    a good king" means',

The door-mouse whispered to me through his epaulette.
    'Things will evolve. You see,
I knew him as a frog, and she's no tailor's dummy.
    Q.E.D.'

Omne Vivum ex Ovo

Like seconds hatching out of minutes from a marbled
    Easter craquelure,
The embryonic beak is inside pecking, nodding like an
    agitated raconteur

Who tells strange tales of mocking-birds and ostriches,
    envelopes and ceiling-wax
That warms your thumb impressed on it, the whorly
    autograph that no one asked

You for: the files contained the fingerprints already.
    Your identity was known
To Principalities and Powers by the guardian reconnaissance
    angel flown

In from God knows where, to hover at your shoulder.
    And the story is about
To break, however garbled, from whatever source,
    however roundabout:

Nothing comes from nothing, and we know that every
    living thing comes from an egg.
The prisoners are standing firm. *Delete.* The renegades
    will not renege.

ALIBI

after Stefan Augustin Doinas

The Words

Yes — someone lived here once. You know it by the pungent
    dragon-whiff,
The way a zephyr blows a ghostly music from those conches,
    like the hieroglyph

Of where we are. The dog-rough breath that slabbered here
    is now a mere miasma,
Baffled that the structure of the universe should be
    corpuscled in its plasma.

Hear? The deep vast stratum of a limestone sea still
    broadcasts sound-waves, and
The guardian angels of its threshold are connected to
    us by an ampersand

When we talk in our sleep. There have been other revenants,
    of course: whole asylums
Of escaped lunatics, diatribes of Vandals reared on horse-
    shit, Crusaders and credendums.

Here, consonants have been eclipsed, and vowels carry
    umlauts, like the moan
Of lovers who repaired here to strip off their shadows
    before swoon-
Ing into one another's arms. Now, it is a reservoir of
    silence, or a Twilight Zone . . .

The Poet as Snow-Merchant

When spring has sprung and disappeared the snow,
　　and youngsters want to laugh at grown-
Ups, but find — instead of snowdrifts — brothers,
　　parents (ready-made folk), then the clown

Appears, this crazy who sells snow. Hibernian winter
　　permafrosts his soul;
He haggles like a lunatic with naked trees, his
　　frozen birds and ice-floes

Creaking like somnivolent Antarctica. He speaks
　　of seeds as unexploded
Atom bombs. Swans drift by in caravanserai across
　　the colour-coded

Blue ice of one eye; you could catch a pike in
　　the pupil-black bullet-hole
Drilled in the other. He hawks his merchandise
　　remorselessly, and being snow

Himself, he spreads himself about: a scattered
　　aftermath of downy pillow-
Feathers marks the progress of his unseen army,
　　in which all the jolly fellows
Carry brooms instead of ostrich plumes; the mayor's statue
　　they denounce as being hollow.

Me and My Cousin

'As for the Archaeopteryx — for such I thought it
    might have been — I hopped on to its neck.
It turned out to be an alabaster blue. Its name was
    really Roc.

Syllables of evening stars becoming Lucifers dropped
    from its beak;
Three deep infernos, funnel-grey, were born within
    its awful look.

Over and above the stratosphere I flew; from noon
    to dewy eve I whirled,
Till I glanced down and noticed it had laid an egg.
    The egg was called The World.'

'Yes,' my cousin said, 'mind you, this Dodo — Roc
    or Archaeopteryx — does not exist.'
'No, it don't,' I answered, as I grappled with its neck,
    'I know it don't exist.'

Alibi

Remorselessly, in fields and forests, on street corners,
    on the eternal
Altar of the bed, murder is done. Was I there? I
    stared into the terminal

Of my own mirrored pupil, and saw my eye denying it,
    like one hand
Washing clean the other. Where was I then? Everybody
    wears the same Cain brand

Emblazoned on their foreheads. I saw the deed and what
    it led to. Heard the shriek
As well. And then my eyes were decommissioned by the knife.
    But I saw him last week,

And I know he is amongst us. And no, I can't tell his
    name. What name would you
Make up for murderers of their own childhood, who
    believe lies to be true?

The lovers enter the marrowbone of a madman and succumb
    slowly in their pit
Of lime. A croaking black unkindness of ravens has
    cloaked it

With a counterfeit of corpses. All our words were in vain.
    What flag are we supposed
To raise above the citadel? Where should we go? All
    the roads are closed.

O ubiquitous surveillant God, we are accomplices to
    all assassinations.
Gag me, choke me, strangle me, and tell me that there
    are no further destinations.

And finally, it must be left unsaid that those not born
    to this, our vampire family,
Sleep soundly in their beds: they have the final alibi.

Bird

No. How should I know what you call that fowl you
      craned your neck towards as it
Scooted overhead? I'd need a Photofit.

For all I know, it has the squawk-box of a coot,
      the awkward stagger
Of a stork. Could it be a Stuka?

Fucked if I know. What dreck does it eat? Does it
      spend life on the wing?
Does it regurgitate? Or sing?

Are the Easter eggs it lays in monasteries egg-shaped?
      Does it wear
Frankincense or myrrh? Or swear?

All I know is this refrain: *Hello, hello, you nightmare
      archipelago,*
I don't know birdshit from guano.

Siege

The fortress balanced on a lance-tip. Unseen army.
    The wells were clogged,
The smoke kept low. We caught the double-headed eagle
    and we ate its mystagogue.

Epidemics came and went. Familiar atavistic ghosts
    kept firing arrows
From the parapets into the world beyond. Nothing.
    Only the stars

In the wound in the side of the god. Then treason struck
    at midnight and the gate
Capitulated. Cowards kow-towed. Nobody. The dazzling
    pirate

Moon broke out. Still nobody. Afflicted by a strange
    disease of sundered
Windows, we weep eternities of blood. There's nobody.
    But we, we have surrendered.

Cortège

I see her on her balcony, the gorgeous fat one,
    slobbering over mandarins
And shivering with laughter, scattering confetti to
    the March winds'

Desultory snowflakes. Meanwhile, down here in The Square,
    three young troubadours
Are cuffed and collared to a rocking tumbril, drawn not
    by horses

But by out-of-breath philosophers. Wooden drum-wheels
    hooped with argent
Rumble towards the scaffold. Unleavened breadcrumbs lie
    crushed on the pavement.

Like two crawling barbed-wire hedges, halberdiers
    conduct a parallel
On either side. Their pikes are glittering with geometry
    and frost. It's cold as hell.

The News

Mouse hopping from mouth to mouth:

For all those child-like souls who crept on all fours
    through loopholes in the city wall;
For deserters from the wars, all drenched in sweat and
    dust beneath their chain-mail;

For the hired assassins crying out for baptism, for
    those historians, provocateurs
Of songs and riddles, who preserve the myth in
    annotated airs;

For the brief reign of kings who only have an hour
    to go; for mothers-to-be
Who hide their embryos in wombs until they pick
    their time and place to be;

For the epileptics, in whom Lucifer has been condemned
    to genuflect
Forever twitching; for those guided by a star; for
    that Byzantine sect

Whose bishops' ears are stuffed with ceremonial
    cotton wool, who chant of hope
Because they suffer the *ennui* of knowing God;
    for the Romish Pope;

For those wingèd choirs of Pandemonium and Princip-
    alities; for movie queens
All spellbound by their beauty to the millions gazing
    at the silent screens;

For all those quacks who speculate in pain; for
    long-dead Draculas
Who re-appear in snap-shot family portraits; for the
    miraculous

Ontology of life in other galaxies, and all their
    bat-eared aliens;
And even for myself, the self-deluded author of these
    simple lines:

See me, riding on my spitfire stallion, just back from
    the fairy-story
Where it grazed on live coals: *Everyone, please hear
The News! Believe my story!*

The meeting has been cancelled! This, by word of mouth!

A Pair

All human kind deserves love. But the lunatic who tries
    to plait a rope
Of sand in order to lasso the newly-risen moon, and by
    this trope

Be levitated; the other dope who, stooped over a river of
    gold, spends all
His life in moulding it to the shape of the faceless wind,
    to give us all

A newly-minted coinage: this odd pair can hitch themselves
    to my star
Any time. And when I'm not at home, you'll know for sure
    they are.

OPERA

for Marlyn Beck
and Philip Hammond

Alpha

Our Camel squadron took off in an *A* formation so as
    not to be
Confused with a skein of geese. We raised our hands in
    signs of *V* for Victory

And honked our rubber bulb-horns in a parped anticipation
    of our recon-
Naissance. Goggled, snorkled, gauntletted, we ran the
    gamut of *sine qua non*.

Baron von Richthofen swooped out of the sun in his red
    Fokker tri-plane,
Writing cursive loops and firing hyphen-guns. Three of
    us made up a quatrain

Dog-fight, till our airy armies swam together like an
    alphabet in soup,
Or stars embroidered on the blue veil of Our Lady
    of Guadaloupe;

Remote among the clouds above, we sparred like Montagues
    and Capulets.
They shot blank verse at us. We answered with a shower
    of rhyming couplets.

Bravo

A major-domo barred the door, all false-teeth epaulettes
and braid,
Uniform fire-engine red. I tipped a nod and wink
to him, and left the rest unsaid.

He swept off his hat. The big vermilion heart of him
engrossed his body, till its core
Became him, though he still maintained his hands, with
which he opened up himself — cantor

Of the ventricles and arteries — and sang my entrance.
I stepped into the atrium.
Above me, the sky of the mouth. Below, the floor of
the tongue. Then, Byzantium

Of vocal chords and larynx. Bee-loud glades of business.
Trojan horses
Whinnying, yet reined in by their constables. Words of
retribution and remorse

Buzzed across the city. Video advertisements for peace.
Talk about the futures
Of uninfibulated lips, how they would take a scissors
to our sutures.

Charlie

'Oscar the Dog' had 'gone out for a walk', so it was
    up to Charlie to stand in.
Loaded Lüger by his side, he lay upon a gold-black
    bale of cannabin.

Since this was in the Southern hemisphere, the stars
    were all the wrong way round.
There, water gurgled into unplugged plug-holes with
    an anti-clockwise sound.

The pre-War pick-up truck drove up and stopped and
    shuddered till its lights went off.
Car doors creaked. Men got out. The radio was playing
    Rimsky-Korsakov.

The twin volcanoes — Balalaika, Karaoke — rumbled
    grumpily.
Stars poured down in bucketsful. Chuck reacted rather
    jumpily,

And shot before shot at. He was cut into a thousand
    by a Triad
In a hemisemidemiquaver, while the wireless played
    Schéhérazade.

Delta

The blues they make down there come out of Mason jars
    and sinsemilla cigarettes,
The hollers of the whippoorwill, the clicking of cicadas'
    castanets.

They have sold their souls to many devils. They're
    the alcohol in syllabub.
They phrase their wired-up twelve-bar syllables with
    accents of Beelzebub.

Broken bottle-necks are popular for stabbing, or for
    sliding on steel strings.
A knife would do as well, as, hunched over his azure
    guitar, the blind man sings

Of doom and gloom, of snakes in rooms, the various uses
    of a coffee-spoon,
Of sugar, tea, and locks, and keys, how everything goes
    mostly to this tune:

Woke up this morning, blues were on my mind. I put the
    record on. It wouldn't go.
I pulled up the blind. The sunlight was too loud.
    I put on shades of indigo.

Echo

Baffled by the earphones stereoed into my labyrinthine
    intervention,
I cupped them to me for what seemed like an infinitely
    long span of attention.

Trying to skat along with it, my tongue got tied in knots —
    Thumb Knots, Marlin Spikes
And Sheepshanks — and it struck me that the jazz had been
    recorded on two mono mikes.

It struck me like a bell that Charlie Parker often parked
    his saxophone
In pawn-shops while he mained the 'horse' into his veins
    while sitting on the 'throne'.

The sax's bell was beaten gold, like some enormously
    expensive lavatory bowl;
Ensconced in Caesar's 'Little Palace', he shot the bop
    into the heart of Soul.

Diminishing thirteenths cascaded by. The faulty springs
    were tautened by elastic bands.
My fingers were all ears and thumbs. I listened to
    the span of Charlie Parker's hands.

Foxtrot

Syncopated like a panto horse's hooves when changing
    down from trot to walk,
I undertook the delicate negotiations, talking rot instead
    of talk.

I played my cards, and kept the guns below the table
    in their make-believe;
We were not playing with the full deck, since the Ace
    of Spades was up a sleeve.

I saw its black heart pinned to a barn door, drilled
    through by a single bullet
In some imaginary marksman showdown, commemorated in
    this ballad

Where the hero is your two-track Hood, who robs to give
    the poor some Tuck.
Robin's Zeno's arrow hit the Zen-spot. The Sheriff
    thought it was a spot of luck.

Not so. It was on the cards. They didn't even spot the
    polka-dotted horse.
I shuffled hands and footsteps as the wireless played
    a minuet of Morse.

Golf

But really, Xanadu is something else, I was drawling
    at the nineteenth hole:
We were drinking 'Milk of Paradise'. The juke-box
    pumped us full of rock 'n' roll.

I gnawed my green olive to its stone and spat the pip
    into a fingerbowl,
Into the stubbed-out crisps and cigarette-butts. We
    spoke a rigmarole

Of lakes, putts, troughs, fairways, bunkers, greens,
    trees, hazards, tees, the principles
Of golf-ball aeronautics, the difference between
    the various dimples and pimples,

Bogeys, eagles, albatrosses. Alf complained about
    his handicap,
That he'd been born eighteen drinks ahead. He shakily
    unscrewed a hub-cap

Of cocaine. Suddenly, we both took short. He followed me
    into the Gents.
We snorted it like three Wise Men whose brains were shot
    with gold, and myrrh, and frankincense.

Hotel

I jiggled the jiggery-pokery key in the lock of Room
    Two Hundred and Seven.
The bed was unmade. Six Silk Cut butts in the ashtray.
    A Seventh Heaven

This was not. I crashed out anyway. The nylon-sheeted
    mirror aura of my pre-
Decessor wrapped me in its Turin shroud. Everything
    seemed redolent of Brie.

I dozed until the chambermaid's annunciation. She
    badly wanted to 'make
Up' my room. She simply had to change the unused
    towels. I got showered wide awake

And strolled down to the bar into the wall-to-wall,
    cool-filtered Muzak.
It was packed with businessmen, gesticulating in their
    bookies' tic-tac.

Much later — six or so night-porter's miniatures
    beneath my belt — I loomed
Upstairs. Unlocked a door. A suit lay on the bed.
    Not mine. Whose was this room?

India

Larger than life, the Empress of India sat enthroned
    in the stoned foyer
Of the Royal Victoria Hospital. I was looking for
    the 'X-Ray

Department', and the Empress didn't have the answer,
    though she had a handy
Way with orb and sceptre. And her green bronze gaze
    did not include Mahatma Ghandi.

I stubbed out my cigarette-butt on her plinth and walked
    right through the heavy-duty
Blasted-polythene swing doors. There sat Mahatma in
    a nappy dhoti,

Holding his two arms at one arm's length apart, as if
    a mother wound a skein
Of wool on them. *You want to talk?* I answered, *Can you
bring me to Sinn Féin?*

The volunteer lay on the bed. His dark glasses still on.
    His Armalite beside.
I just about made out his skeleton. I tried to prise
    some peace from him. Then he died.

Juliet

I met him in Verona Market, fingering the oranges
  and the greens.
He seemed interested in local produce. We were into
  Kings and Queens.

I bought a bunch of thyme. He bought rue. Our hands
  touched. I was contagious to a Montague,
And the grand piazza was pizzaz with heraldry emblazoned
  in a rendezvous

Of factions: oriflammes and banderoles, standards,
  swallowtails and bannerettes,
All fluttering with shamrocks, roses, thistles, high
  above the parapets

Where guzzling trumpeters tilted trumpets to their lips
  like bottles full of Coke
Or dope-imbibers gazing at the ceiling, relishing their
  skywriting smoke.

We called the song they played 'Our Song'. I thought
  together we would be, perhaps.
But the Montagues put on their cloaks, the Capulets
  put on their caps.

Kilo

The *Sûreté* had guaranteed the operation would be covert,
    low-key,
Hunky-dory, under wraps, each detail okey-dokey as
    synecdoche;

You recognise the Citröen by its wheels? That's what
    I mean: the part
Denotes the smoky whole, especially when played by
    Humphrey Bogart.

A car-klaxon blew a foggy Gauloise note of pianissimo
    accordion bass
Droned out across an empty ballroom floor; the dancers
    were in hyperspace.

The foreign freighter creaked its starry moorings. Frogmen
    swam up through a galaxy,
Synchronized like watches. The rendezvous would happen
    in a Falls Road taxi.

Paki Black, Red Leb, and Acupulco Gold: dogs sniffed
    the aromatic rainbow.
Maigret blew a cloud of briar smoke and spoke: *Lo-Ki?*
    Kilo? O.K! K.O!

Lima

By covert way of bugs in bags, and cameras in mikes
    and lapel butt-
On holes, through scam and zoom in hotel rooms, the
    case was open and shut.

Editing it, we put a lot of jump cuts in. Otherwise,
    you would be watching
Paint dry, so to speak. With reconnaissance slice and splice,
    what we're about is catching

Someone in an icon act of giving or receiving. We
    move in on that,
Especially when llama trains descend the Andes and
    emerge in Laundromat.

We've got their bleats all taped, explaining to each other
    how the 'Lima beans'
Turn into rocks of crack or coke. If you ask me, they're
    a bunch of hashasheens.

From his black alpaca coat, Inspector Morse took out
    his Baedeker and fount-
Ain pen. He unscrewed the mosaic tortoiseshell. Then
    he wrote this skewed account.

Mike

The trump or jew's harp is a great 'accomplishment',
    especially when fed
Into the jaws of a Mike, who twangs and amplifies it
    with his knucklehead.

It buzzes from the cavern of the mouth, and resonates
    its bit between the teeth:
Didgeridoo, parlante, intermezzo, pizzicato, it reminds
    me of Pádraig O'Keeffe,

Who used to phrase his fiddling of 'Rocking the Cradle'
    with a latch-key
Clenched between his non-existent dentures; more often
    than not, he'd be on the spree.

It sounded like a doll's cry, emanating from the
    sound-box in its back,
As you bed it down and watch its eyes roll shut into
    their cul-de-sac . . .

Just now, I heard an elephant trump some two miles
    down the road from Belfast Zoo,
And it struck me with the force of logic, that a jaw's
    harp is a much superior kazoo.

November

Yellow fog converged implacably against the cold damp
   window-pane. Sherlock
Had just shot up and was fiddling with a languid fantasia
   on a Bartok

Theme. Watson tried to do the crossword, but the clues
   were fiendishly difficult.
The fog was Wordsmith's 'Daffodils', or saffron as the
   garments of a cult.

The great sleuth stuffed his big blow-pipe full of the aromatic
   acrid black shag mix
And puffed a fug across the upstairs room in Morse of nicotine
   and hieroglyphics.

Jaundice, mustard, amber was the smog. The doctor dug into
   a pot of Mrs Hudson's marmalade,
Perusing out the wisps of rind. He hummed a few bars
   of 'The White Cockade'.

The detective measured up his hypodermic for a second jag,
   and found a vein.
Watson turned to the 'Agony' column. *I say, Holmes!*
   he said. But Holmes was entering Cockaigne.

Oscar

I held the figurine aloft, revelling in my actor's
    gravestone smile;
I boldly faced an orchestra of flash, as paparazzi
    packed the aisle.

I thanked everyone: all those who'd made it possible
    for me to be,
Down to the midwife and my grade-school teacher; my
    analyst; the Committee;

Not forgetting William Shakespeare, who had writ the
    script on vellum,
Nor the born anachronist director, who had set it in
    the *ante bellum* —

The way he saw it, Hamlet was a kind of Southern dude
    who chewed cheroots.
He wanted Vivien to play Ophelia Leigh. The uncle
    was a *putz*.

So, everybody, give a big hand to *All Our Yesterdays*,
    this apron weft
And warp of life we strut upon a brief while, till *All
    exeunt, stage left.*

Papa

Emerging from *La Traviata*, the Princess was surrounded
    by a pack of pap-
Arazzi, zapping her with antiquated flashbacks. In a chromium
    hub-cap

Of the limousine, I saw it all reflected, the fish-eye lens
    distort-
Ed by her Bambi look, her handbag's patent *noir*, her
    skirt of ultra-short.

Bespoke aides engaged each others' walkie-talkies,
    quacking to the marksmen on their roof-
Top high. The windows of the cabriolet whirred up
    their smoked-glass bulletproof.

A suddenly-jumped-up, up-braided major-domo opened
    the car door.
She jack-knifed herself in. There sat the other Princess
    with her mobile semaphore.

Hands in gloves, they yakked of *l'ancien règime*, when
    they had often asked what they would be,
And Papa'd snorted in his Mafioso way, *We'll see, Kay.
Sara, we'll see.*

Quebec

We were to recognize each other by a known code of
    buttonhole
And that day's copy of *Le Monde*. They'd flown me straight
    in from out of Charles de Gaulle.

But then, he doesn't show. It's two hours later and
    I'm standing with the oxblood
Briefcase at my feet, attached to me by mental leash,
    when this black hood

Appears from nowhere on his cool-dude blades. He's
    got a yellow Walkman on.
He passes me this folded Rizla, then glides off like
    he was made of teflon.

I opened it to see the message was in mirror, so
    I took it to the Gents.
Briefcase at my feet, I peed, then read the paper's
    looking-glass intelligence:

Names, numbers, sources, drachms, minims, scruples.
    Methadone and moonstone.
I got into a booth to contact them, and opened up
    the book of Anglophone.

Romeo

Romeo was not built in a day, not to speak of Romulus
    or Remus —
Cain and Abel — why Protestants are called Billy — and
    Catholics are Seamus.

It took a school lab labyrinth of history to produce
    these garbled notes
In careful fountain-pen. The arrowed maps of North and South,
    the essays filled with quotes:

The emptied jam-jar full of frog-spawn, blooping on
    the window-sill;
The tapioca of school meals; the sandwiches of squashed
    Norwegian sild;

John West in his sou'wester; *Vesta* matches in their
    yellow box, the *Swift* in blue;
The Orange lily and the Shamrock green; shades of Capulet
    and Montague —

It's all a tangled tagliatelle linguini Veronese that
    I'm trying to unravel
From its strands of DNA and language. Perhaps I need
    a spirit level.

Sierra

The Great American Bald-headed Reconnaissance Eagle
    dwindled in its spiral
High above, as we macheted through the Alpine jungle,
    speaking doggerel

To fool the bugs. The glades buzzed loud with sounds
    of killer bees and coffee-beans;
Squawk-box parrots flitted in and out like cunningly-
    constructed gold machines;

Cappuccino monkeys abounded in the trees, high on
    intravenous caffeine.
Ever upwards, through the chaparral, till we attained
    a peak in Darien,

We struggled. Then we rubbed our eyes: a whole Pacific-
    ful of stars lay spread
Beneath our feet. We tried to read its horoscope, till
    Cortez, like a pot-head,

Spoke out loud and bold: 'I hereby name the various
    dopes of Mexico —
Chimborazo, Cotopaxi, Acapulco and *Sierra del Fuego.*'

Tango

It's all long steps and pauses, where the woman uses
    the man as a crutch;
Ironically, it is unlikely that it comes from the Latin
    verb 'to touch'.

It is not the foxtrot nor the frug, still less the polka-dot
    or rigadoon;
Zapateado, tarantella, rhumba, mambo, allemande, it's not.
    It is a swoon

Of music, castanetted by the clicking silver buttons
    of the square bandoneon,
Which is its instrument, bass-and-treble toned
    like the chameleon:

Beautiful gloomy levity of camouflage, like when
    the girl's bolero
Creaks against the moustachioed starched shirt, as he
    struts and pansies in torero

Mode. He leans into her quickstep jitterbug. Her legs
    are all akimbo
As he shimmies lower, lower, entering the possibility
    of limbo.

Uniform

I've just put on this borrowed armour: second-hand
   cold freezes my bones — but
Really, I feel cool when putting on the company kit.
   It makes me want to strut.

It straightens up my spine. And you have to get the right
   fit: uniforms do not look good
Loose. Tight is what you want, like body-builders' biro
   veins of condom nude,

Statuesque in stances. Geared, belted, buckled, studded,
   epauletted, butt-
Oned-up, I touch my holster-flap and contemplate my
   regulation gun-butt.

It's matt black as the Ace of Spades. I feel I am its
   Jack; I am its suit,
Elaborate as Kama Sutra in my thigh-high, shiny, leather
   girl-shaped boots.

I like especially to guard the homes of opera stars
   and marchionesses,
To feel emblazoned on my serge the twin lightning
   zig-zags of the S.S.

Victor

Before a trumpet clarion brings the panoply of war
    to mind, the fine duet
Of cor anglais and flute takes on an Alpine clarity.
    The theme is 'L'Alouette'.

Slowly, we get to the core of the matter: the Gruyère
    peasants were revolting.
The Emperor wore iron gloves; theirs was a fragile
    dynasty of Ming

And cuckoo clocks that kept calling at the wrong times;
    the outspoken bird
Was wont to contradict its cogs and ratchets. *Tell*,
    not *Klee*, was The Word.

Will took up his cross-bow like he would a fiddle.
    Tuned her to the cuckoo-
'S two time-worn notes, and played 'La Marseillaise'
    until the cockadoodledoo.

Then he put the first bolt in his belt. The second
    fitted to his string. He shot.
In less time than it takes to tell he hit the pip;
    afterwards, he overthrew the despot.

Whisky

Of how the life of water is distilled to liquid gold;
    how the water of
The Liffey becomes Guinness; how explosive cocktails
    take the name of Molotov;

How the wild mountain thyme blows around the blooming
    heather, and the perfumed smoke
Of poteen rises high into the azure sky; how turf
    is the conducive agent, and not coke;

How coke is crack, not heroin, nor smack; how marijuana
    is *La Cucuracha*,
Maryjane, or blow; how many States of mind there are in
    Appalachia;

How you turn into an insect overnight, or after-hours,
    from eating
Magic mushrooms; how the psilocybin got your brain and
    led to some 'Strange Meeting';

How the tongue gets twisted, how 'barbarian' is everyone
    who is not Greek;
How things are named by any other name except themselves,
    thereof I meant to speak.

X-Ray

The faces of the disappeared in blown-up, blurred
  wedding photographs;
The bombing of the Opera House; my lost wall map
  of Belfast; the pikestaffs

Spiked with rebels' decomposing heads; the long-since
  rotted hempen rope;
The razor-wire; the Confidential Telephone; the walls
  that talk of *Fuck the Pope*;

The dragons' teeth; the look-out towers; the body
  politic surveillances;
The terrorist, the might-have-been of half-forgotten,
  long-abandoned chances:

All these are nothing to the blinks and blanks of night's
  inscrutable eternity, which stars
The Northern sky with camp-fire palimpsests of ancient
  wars;

Or these are nothing to the cerebral activity of any
  one of us who sets in train
These zig-zags, or the brain-cells decomposing in some
  rebel brain.

Yankee

I doodled on my flute: some phrases from a half-remembered
    marching-tune étude
Which summoned up a panoply of orange and purple
    oriflammes, the rectitude

Of gleaming ceremonial swords and bowler-hatted cohorts,
    insignia of compasses
And pyramids, all shimmered in the July heat. I wore
    my new dark glasses'

Incognito, being from the other side. I kept my mouth shut,
    so to speak;
I feared my syllables of shibboleth would be interpreted
    as Greek.

Pickpocketlike, I mingled with the crowd and felt its
    huge identity
Of Ulster crush around me. I became a pocket of an
    absolute nonentity . . .

I ran into this guy last night who knew the tune. He
    played it on his Cordovox.
Its name? According to Melodeonman, 'The Battle of
    Appomattox'.

Zulu

At last, I remember the half-broomstick assegai with which
    I used to kill
Imaginary soldiers. I danced around them like a hound
    of Baskerville.

I faced the typecast phalanxes of English, shielded only
    by a dustbin-
Lid; sometimes, I'd *sotto voce* whistle 'The Dragoons
    of Inniskillin',

Till an Agincourt of arrows overwhelm'd me, shot by
    Milton, Keats and Shakespeare,
And I became a redskin, foraging behind the alphabetic
    frontier.

Pale boldface wagons drew themselves into a hurried
    O of barricade;
Mounted on my hobby-horse, I whooped so much, I had
    to take a slug of orangeade.

I loved its cold-jolt glug and fizz, tilted bottle up-
    held like a trumpet
To the sun; or so it might be, in the gargled doggerel
    of this dumb poet.

Notes

The following definitions can be found in *Chambers Twentieth Century Dictionary*:

page 39 Auditque vocatus Apollo: and Apollo hears when invoked — Virgil, *Georg.*, IV. 7

page 40 Solvitur ambulando: (the problem of the reality of motion) is solved by walking, by practical experiment, by actual performance

page 41 Vox et praeterea nihil: a voice and nothing more (of a nightingale)

page 42 Graecum est: non legitur: this is Greek: it is not read (placed against a Greek word in mediaeval MSS., a permission to skip the hard words)

page 43 Par nobile fratrum: a noble pair of brothers — Horace, *Sat.* II, iii, 243

page 44 Jacta est alea: the die is cast (quoted as said by Caesar at the crossing of the Rubicon)

page 45 Aquila non capit muscas: an eagle does not catch flies.

page 46 Cave quid dicis, quando, et cui: beware what you say, when, and to whom

page 47 Labuntur et imputantur: (the moments) slip away and are laid to our account

page 48 Quod erat demonstrandum: or Q.E.D., which was to be proved or demonstrated

page 49 Omne vivum ex ovo: every living thing comes from an egg — attributed to Harvey.

Acknowledgements

Letters from the Alphabet was published in a limited, signed edition to mark the 25th anniversary of The Gallery Press, 6 February 1995.

The versions from the Romanian of Stefan Augustin Doinas were commissioned by John Fairleigh and appeared in *When the Tunnels Meet*, an anthology of contemporary Romanian poetry edited by him (Bloodaxe Books, 1996). I am grateful to Simion Dumitrache and Heather Brett for their literal translations.

Some of the poems also appeared in *Poetry* (Chicago), *Sport* (New Zealand) and '25' (The Gallery Press).